Cute vs. Cute

Who's the Cutest of Them All?

By Barb N. Glossett

Cute vs. Cute is produced by becker&mayer!
11120 NE 33rd Place, Suite 101
Bellevue, WA 98004
www.beckermayer.com

ISBN 978-1-60380-248-2

10 9 8 7 6 5 4 3 2 1   12 13 14 15 16

12020

Editor: Ben Grossblatt
Designer: Megan Sugiyama
Photo Researcher: Jessica Eskelsen
Production Coordinator: Tom Miller
Managing Editor: Michael del Rosario

Photo credits: Front cover and Title page: Bichon frise © Medvedev Andry/Shutterstock; Grey kitten © Utekhina Anna/Shutterstock; little princess diadem © ILeysen/Shutterstock; gold crown © iadams/Shutterstock. Page 3: Chinchilla © Eric Isselée/Shutterstock; Lab puppy © Eric Isselée/Shutterstock; Panda © GlobalP/iStockphoto. Page 4: Guinea pig © Joanna Wnuk/Shutterstock. Page 5: Bunny © Lepas/Shutterstock. Page 6: Duckling © Tischenko Irina/Shutterstock. Page 7: Penguin © Eric Isselée/Shutterstock. Page 8: Raccoon © Eric Isselée/Shutterstock. Page 9: Hedgehog © Eric Isselée/Shutterstock. Page 10: Leopard cub © Eric Isselée/Shutterstock. Page 11: Lab puppy © Eric Isselée/Shutterstock. Page 12: Chipmunk © Eric Isselée/Shutterstock. Page 13: Chinchilla © Eric Isselée/Shutterstock. Page 14: Orangutan © Eric Isselée/Shutterstock. Page 15: Sloth © Eric Isselée/Shutterstock. Page 16: Panda © GlobalP/iStockphoto. Page 17: Gray kitten © Tsekhmister/Shutterstock. Page 18: Tapir © Colin Edwards Photography/Shutterstock. Page 19: Piglet © oksana2010/Shutterstock. Page 20: Lion cub © Eric Isselée/Shutterstock. Page 21: Otter © Eric Isselée/Shutterstock. Page 22: Zebra © Justin Black/Shutterstock. Page 23: Giraffe © Athol Abrahams/Shutterstock. Page 24: Koala © Eric Isselée/Shutterstock. Page 25: Red panda © Eric Isselée/Shutterstock. Page 26: Goat kid © Eric Isselée/Shutterstock. Page 27: Red fox © Eric Isselée/Shutterstock. Page 28: Dwarf hamster © Smit/Shutterstock. Page 29: Wood mouse © Eric Isselée/Shutterstock. Page 30: Fawn © Eric Isselée/Shutterstock. Page 31: Ostrich © Eric Isselée/Shutterstock. Page 32: Lamb © April Turner/Shutterstock. Page 33: Wolf pup © Eric Isselée/Shutterstock. Page 34: Harp seal © FloridaStock/Shutterstock. Page 35: Polar bear © Vishnevskiy Vasily/Shutterstock. Page 36: Elephant © Four Oaks/Shutterstock. Page 37: Wallaroo © Eric Isselée/Shutterstock. Page 38: Red squirrel © Eric Isselée/Shutterstock. Page 39: SIAMESE kitten © Chepko Danil Vitalevich/Shutterstock. Page 40: Shar Pei puppy © Dmitry Kalinovsky/Shutterstock. Page 41: Ferret © Eric Isselée/Shutterstock. Page 42: Donkey © Eric Isselée/Shutterstock. Page 43: Miniature horse © Ron Rowan Photography/Shutterstock. Page 44: Gibbon © Eric Isselée/Shutterstock. Page 45: Spider monkey © Eric Isselée/Shutterstock. Page 46: Tiger cub © Eric Isselée/Shutterstock. Page 47: Sea lion © Eric Isselée/Shutterstock. Page 48: Leopard cub © Eric Isselée/Shutterstock; Gray kitten © Tsekhmister/Shutterstock. Design elements (throughout): animal faces © JungleOutThere/Shutterstock. Back cover: Duckling © Tischenko Irina/Shutterstock; Penguin © Eric Isselée/Shutterstock.

LET THE CUTENESS BEGIN!

Get ready for the most lovable animals ever as they go head-to-head in the ultimate contest: Who's cuter?

A panel of experts has rated these 44 cuties in terms of **Fluzz** (how fluffy-and-fuzzy they are), **Face** (how adorable their little faces are), **Chub** (how roly-poly and pudgy they are), and **Wobble** (how unsteady and precious they are when they walk). These animals are so cute, we had to invent a few other new words to describe them, as well.

Stickers in the back let you tag your favorites and crown your own King and Queen of Cute!

Tiny floppy ears!

Guinea pig

Guinea pigs are loved for their squeezability and all the cute sounds they make: They *wheek* when excited, purr when content, and chirp when hungry.

8	🦁🦁🦁🦁🦁🦁🦁🦁	Fluzz
9	🐵🐵🐵🐵🐵🐵🐵🐵🐵	Face
7	🐷🐷🐷🐷🐷🐷🐷	Chub
5	🐧🐧🐧🐧🐧	Wobble

That nose! It wiggles!

Bunny

Happy bunnies do a quick, springy dance step called a binky. A bunny's hobbies include chewing stuff and digging.

Fluzz	🦁🦁🦁🦁🦁🦁🦁🦁🦁	9
Face	🐵🐵🐵🐵🐵🐵🐵	7
Chub	🐷🐷🐷🐷🐷🐷🐷🐷	8
Wobble	🐧🐧🐧🐧🐧	5

Flat, flappy feet!

Duckling

Their bills are rubbery. Their bottoms are waddly.
When they hatch, they fall in love with the first big
thing they see, which is usually Mama.

7	🐑🐑🐑🐑🐑🐑🐑	Fluzz
6	🐵🐵🐵🐵🐵🐵	Face
6	🐷🐷🐷🐷🐷🐷	Chub
8	🐧🐧🐧🐧🐧🐧🐧🐧	Wobble

So fluffish!

I want one

Penguin chick

After their waterproof feathers come in, penguins become sleek swimmers. But when they're born, baby penguins are clumsy little puffballs.

Fluzz		7
Face		5
Chub		7
Wobble		10

Sneaky hands!

Raccoon kit

Raccoons are smart and curious, and they love to climb trees. Raccoons can live just about anywhere, from forests to cities, as long as they're near water.

7	🦁🦁🦁🦁🦁🦁🦁	Fluzz
9	🐵🐵🐵🐵🐵🐵🐵🐵🐵	Face
5	🐱🐱🐱🐱🐱	Chub
4	🐧🐧🐧🐧	Wobble

Hedgehog

Everything about him is pokey, from his tiny claws to his pointy ears and the prickles all over his back. Did you know baby hedgies are called hoglets?

Fluzz	🦁🦁🦁🦁	**4**
Face	🐵🐵🐵🐵🐵🐵🐵	**7**
Chub	🐷🐷🐷🐷🐷	**5**
Wobble	🐧🐧🐧🐧🐧🐧	**6**

Totally fuzzy ears!

So fuzzy!

Leopard cub

Leopard cubs look like they're wearing spotted pj's.
They love to play, spending hours tumbling on top of
their brothers and sisters.

8		Fluzz
9		Face
5		Chub
4		Wobble

Labrador puppy

It's the dog that's part duck! (Kind of.) To help them swim and play in the water, Labradors have webbed toes and special fur.

Fluzz	🐑🐑🐑🐑🐑🐑	6
Face	🐵🐵🐵🐵🐵🐵🐵🐵🐵	9
Chub	🐷🐷🐷🐷	4
Wobble	🐧🐧🐧🐧🐧🐧	6

Chipmunk

Chipmunks gather food in woodsy areas and use their furry cheeks like shopping bags. They dig big burrows and pile up their food inside.

8	🦁🦁🦁🦁🦁🦁🦁🦁	**Fluzz**
7	🐵🐵🐵🐵🐵🐵🐵	**Face**
5	🐷🐷🐷🐷🐷	**Chub**
4	🐧🐧🐧🐧	**Wobble**

Chinchilla

Like other rodents, chinchillas need to keep chew-chew-chewing or else their teeth will grow too darn big. "Chinnies" have velvety coats and fluffety tails.

Fluzz		7
Face		6
Chub		7
Wobble		6

The faces it makes!

Orangutan

These sturdy apes have long red hair. Even though grown-up orangutans can weigh as much as grown-up people, they sleep in tree nests every night.

6	🦁🦁🦁🦁🦁🦁	Fluzz
8	🐵🐵🐵🐵🐵🐵🐵🐵	Face
5	🐱🐱🐱🐱🐱	Chub
4	🐧🐧🐧🐧	Wobble

14

Sloth

Sloths are super slowpokes that spend most of their time hanging upside down in trees. They like to stay curled up in a ball way up high.

Fluzz	🦁🦁🦁🦁🦁🦁🦁	7
Face	🐵🐵🐵🐵🐵🐵🐵🐵	8
Chub	🐷🐷🐷🐷🐷🐷	6
Wobble	🐧🐧🐧🐧🐧🐧	6

This one!

Panda cub

A newborn panda weighs about as much as an apple, but it's a lot fuzzier. Pandas eat bamboo for breakfast, lunch, dinner. . . and snacks!

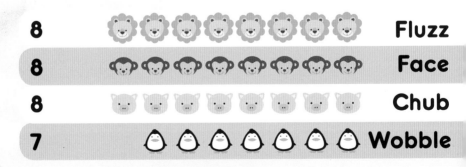

8		Fluzz
8		Face
8		Chub
7		Wobble

Tabby kitten

Kittens, like this stripy tabby, are natural-born students. They watch their moms to learn to wash themselves and to play stalky-pouncey games.

Fluzz	🐺🐺🐺🐺🐺🐺🐺🐺🐺	9
Face	🐵🐵🐵🐵🐵🐵🐵🐵🐵	9
Chub	🐱🐱🐱🐱🐱🐱	6
Wobble	🐧🐧🐧🐧🐧🐧	6

Speckles!

Tapir

It looks like someone crossed an anteater with an elephant. A tapir uses its wiggling mini-trunk for sniffing. The babies, like this one, have streaky spots.

3	🦁🦁🦁	Fluzz
6	🐵🐵🐵🐵🐵🐵	Face
4	🐷🐷🐷🐷	Chub
5	🐧🐧🐧🐧🐧	Wobble

Snouty snuffles!

Piglet

Pigs are smart and grunty. Some pigs are such good smellers they can sniff mushrooms that live underground.

Fluzz		5
Face		7
Chub		7
Wobble		6

Spotty
head!

Lion cub

To say *hello*, lions like to lick and butt their heads
against their friends. Lion cubs can be real nuzzlers.
The brave ones playfully nip at Dad's tail.

8	😺😺😺😺😺😺😺😺	Fluzz
9	🐵🐵🐵🐵🐵🐵🐵🐵🐵	Face
6	🐷🐷🐷🐷🐷🐷	Chub
5	🐧🐧🐧🐧🐧	Wobble

Otter

Otters love slip-sliding down muddy banks into the water. These otters can handle things easily with their clever paws.

Fluzz	🦁🦁🦁🦁🦁🦁	6
Face	🐵🐵🐵🐵🐵🐵🐵🐵	8
Chub	🐷🐷🐷🐷🐷🐷🐷	7
Wobble	🐧🐧🐧🐧🐧🐧	6

Those stripy legs!

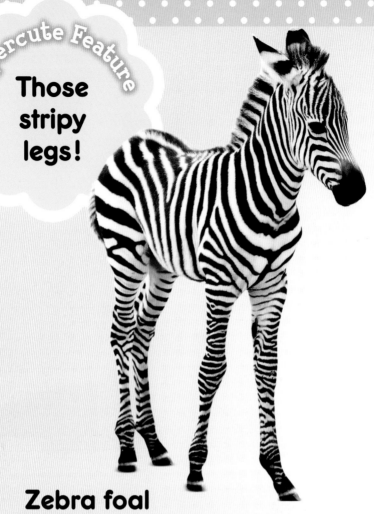

Zebra foal

This zebra is stripy all over. Even the mane of hair down its neck is striped. Newborn zebras take shaky steps at first, before they get good at walking.

3	🦁🦁🦁	**Fluzz**
5	🐵🐵🐵🐵🐵	**Face**
3	🐷🐷🐷	**Chub**
7	🐧🐧🐧🐧🐧🐧🐧	**Wobble**

Giraffe calf

The calves start out small (well, small for *giraffes*), but they don't stay that way for long. A giraffe calf can grow as much as an inch in a day!

Fluzz	🦁🦁🦁	**3**
Face	🐵🐵🐵🐵🐵	**5**
Chub	🐷🐷🐷	**3**
Wobble	🐧🐧🐧🐧🐧🐧🐧	**7**

23

Frizzy ears!

#1

Koala

Koalas are sleepy little fuzzies that rest 18 hours a day. Most other animals can't stand koala food—eucalyptus leaves—so koalas don't have to share.

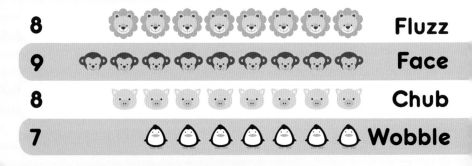

8		Fluzz
9		Face
8		Chub
7		Wobble

Red panda

To keep their woolly coats clean and fluffy, red pandas give themselves long baths. They snooze in tree nests and climb down headfirst.

Fluzz	🦁🦁🦁🦁🦁🦁🦁🦁🦁	9
Face	🐵🐵🐵🐵🐵🐵🐵🐵🐵	9
Chub	🐷🐷🐷🐷🐷🐷🐷	7
Wobble	🐧🐧🐧🐧🐧🐧🐧	7

Nubby horn nubbins!

Goat

Baby goats, called kids, are famous for their playfulness. They're so frisky there's a special word that means "acting like a happy goat": capering!

7		Fluzz
6		Face
4		Chub
5		Wobble

Red fox

Fox kits are jumpy critters. Their thick, fluffy tails are called brushes, maybe because they're so long they sometimes brush the ground.

Fluzz	🦁🦁🦁🦁🦁🦁🦁🦁	8
Face	🐵🐵🐵🐵🐵🐵🐵🐵	8
Chub	🐷🐷🐷🐷	4
Wobble	🐧🐧🐧🐧	4

Dwarf hamster

A dwarf hamster is a teeny fluffins—even teenier than the regular kind of hamster. All hamsters store food for later in their big cheek pouches.

8	🦁🦁🦁🦁🦁🦁🦁🦁	Fluzz
7	🐵🐵🐵🐵🐵🐵🐵	Face
8	🐷🐷🐷🐷🐷🐷🐷🐷	Chub
6	🐧🐧🐧🐧🐧🐧	Wobble

Pink hands and feet!

Wood mouse

During the nights in really cold weather, wood mice turn into dozy little lazies. When the weather warms up and they want to go fast, they hop!

Fluzz	🦁🦁🦁🦁🦁🦁	6
Face	🐵🐵🐵🐵🐵🐵🐵	7
Chub	🐷🐷🐷🐷🐷🐷🐷	7
Wobble	🐧🐧🐧🐧🐧🐧	6

Knobbly legs!

Fawn

Fawns are baby deer. These speckled little things can walk almost as soon as they're born, but they're pretty stumbly at first.

5	🐑🐑🐑🐑🐑	Fluzz
8	🐵🐵🐵🐵🐵🐵🐵🐵	Face
3	🐷🐷🐷	Chub
8	🐧🐧🐧🐧🐧🐧🐧🐧	Wobble

Messy, mussy feathers!

Ostrich

When they're all grown up, ostriches are the biggest, fastest, featheriest birds in the world. And if they get mad, they kick!

Fluzz	🦁🦁🦁🦁🦁	5
Face	🐵🐵🐵🐵🐵	5
Chub	🐷🐷🐷🐷🐷🐷	6
Wobble	🐧🐧🐧🐧🐧🐧	6

Waggly tail!

Lamb

Lambs like to run and kick up their heels. They try to make big jumps, but they can manage only little hops. Lambs really do say, "Baa baa!"

5	🐑🐑🐑🐑🐑	Fluzz
6	🐵🐵🐵🐵🐵🐵	Face
3	🐱🐱🐱	Chub
7	🐧🐧🐧🐧🐧🐧🐧	Wobble

Wolf pup

Wolves are howlers. When they're pups they make long, yippy-yowly puppy howls. At their opposite ends, wolf pups have silly, droopy tails.

Fluzz	🐑🐑🐑🐑🐑🐑🐑	7
Face	🐵🐵🐵🐵🐵🐵🐵🐵	8
Chub	🐷🐷🐷🐷	4
Wobble	🐧🐧🐧🐧🐧	5

Puppy-dog eyes!

Harp seal pup

It's hard getting around on the snow with those flippers, but the pups pull themselves along. They have little whiskers and two dots for eyebrows.

7	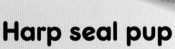	Fluzz
9		Face
7		Chub
7		Wobble

Big, round rump!

Polar bear cub

A polar bear cub is a roly-poly chubbins. One day, it will be gigantic and fierce, but for now it loves to roll in the snow and give playful nips.

Fluzz	🦁🦁🦁🦁🦁🦁🦁	7
Face	🐵🐵🐵🐵🐵🐵🐵🐵🐵	9
Chub	🐷🐷🐷🐷🐷	5
Wobble	🐧🐧🐧🐧🐧	5

Wrinkles all over!

Elephant

One thing about elephants: Even when they're little, they're big. They use their huge ears for fanning themselves and their long trunks for bath-time spraying.

1	🦁	**Fluzz**
6	🐵🐵🐵🐵🐵🐵	**Face**
6	🐷🐷🐷🐷🐷🐷	**Chub**
5	🐧🐧🐧🐧🐧	**Wobble**

Supercute Feature

Fabulastic feet!

Wallaroo

It's not a wallaby. It's not a kangaroo. It's a wallaroo, a cousin of those famous bouncers. A wallaroo's giant tail is a working kickstand.

Fluzz	🦁🦁🦁🦁🦁	5
Face	🐵🐵🐵🐵🐵🐵🐵	7
Chub	🐱🐱🐱🐱	4
Wobble	🐧🐧🐧🐧🐧🐧	6

Bushiest tail ever!

Red squirrel

Except for their fronts, which stay fluffy-white, red squirrels' coats get darker and thicker in the fall. Their tufty ears get even tuftier.

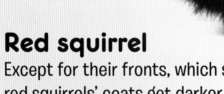

9		Fluzz
6		Face
6		Chub
3		Wobble

Siamese kitten

Siamese cats are downright smudgy. The markings start out light and get darker as the kittens grow up. Siamese cats are loud talkers.

Fluzz	🐑🐑🐑🐑🐑🐑🐑	7
Face	🐵🐵🐵🐵🐵🐵🐵🐵🐵	9
Chub	🐷🐷🐷🐷	4
Wobble	🐧🐧🐧🐧🐧🐧	6

Droopy face!

Shar Pei puppy

Shar Peis are wrinklish dogs with little ears and
blue-black tongues. Shar Peis get less wrinkly as
they grow up. Too bad.

7	🦁🦁🦁🦁🦁🦁🦁	Fluzz
8	🐵🐵🐵🐵🐵🐵🐵🐵	Face
7	🐷🐷🐷🐷🐷🐷🐷	Chub
5	🐧🐧🐧🐧🐧	Wobble

Ferret

Ferrets do a happy, squirmy dance when they want to play. Their raccoony masks make them look like they're up to something. Maybe they are.

Fluzz	🦁🦁🦁🦁🦁🦁🦁	7
Face	🐵🐵🐵🐵🐵🐵🐵	7
Chub	🐷🐷🐷	3
Wobble	🐧🐧🐧🐧	4

Ears stick up!

Donkey

Boy donkey babies are called jacks. Girl donkey babies are called jennys. Baby donkeys walk on their bendy, wiggly legs almost as soon as they're born.

5	🐑🐑🐑🐑🐑	Fluzz
6	🐵🐵🐵🐵🐵🐵	Face
3	🐷🐷🐷	Chub
7	🐧🐧🐧🐧🐧🐧🐧	Wobble

**Big lump
of a nose!**

Miniature horse

Miniature horses are regular horses, only smaller.
Minis will never be as big as other horses, no matter
how old they get. This one has a thick, snuzzly coat.

Fluzz	🐑🐑🐑🐑🐑🐑🐑🐑	8
Face	🐵🐵🐵🐵🐵🐵	6
Chub	🐷🐷🐷🐷🐷🐷🐷	7
Wobble	🐧🐧🐧🐧🐧	5

That little face peeking out!

Gibbon

A gibbon's favorite way of traveling is whooshing from branch to branch high above the ground. Gibbons hold their hands over their heads when they walk.

8	🐑🐑🐑🐑🐑🐑🐑🐑	**Fluzz**
9	🐵🐵🐵🐵🐵🐵🐵🐵🐵	**Face**
3	🐷🐷🐷	**Chub**
4	🐧🐧🐧🐧	**Wobble**

Spider monkey

Little spider monkeys spend most of their first year clinging to Mama or riding on her back. Later, they swing in the trees, using their tails like extra hands.

Fluzz	🐑🐑🐑🐑🐑🐑🐑🐑	8
Face	🐵🐵🐵🐵🐵🐵🐵🐵	8
Chub	🐷🐷🐷🐷	4
Wobble	🐧🐧🐧🐧	4

Pink nose!

Tiger cub

Little tigers are rough and tough. Like other baby cats, they like to nip their playmates and swat things with their paws.

8	🦁🦁🦁🦁🦁🦁🦁🦁	Fluzz
8	🐵🐵🐵🐵🐵🐵🐵🐵	Face
6	🐱🐱🐱🐱🐱🐱	Chub
5	🐧🐧🐧🐧🐧	Wobble

Tiny ear nubbles!

Sea lion pup

Flippery sea lions love sunning themselves, wriggling around on the sand and zooming through the water. They bark, growl, chirp, and click.

Fluzz	🦁🦁🦁🦁	4
Face	🐵🐵🐵🐵🐵🐵	6
Chub	🐱🐱🐱🐱🐱🐱	6
Wobble	🐧🐧🐧🐧🐧🐧🐧	7

The cuteness experts have had their chance to vote, and now it's your turn.

Use the stickers on the following sheet to tag your favorite cute animals.

 Mark the winner of each match up.

 Choose the champions of Fluzz, Face, Chub, and Wobble.

 Select the ultimate King and Queen of Cute.

 Or just decorate the pages any way you like!